Books by Kenneth Koch

DAYS
and
NIGHTS

DAYS and NIGHTS

Kenneth Koch

RANDOM HOUSE
New York

Some of these poems have been previously published in the *New York Arts Journal*,
and *Grand Street*.

Library of Congress Cataloging in Publication Data
Koch, Kenneth,
Days and nights.
I. Title.
PS3521.027D3   1982   811'.54   82-40128
ISBN 0-394-52480-2   AACR2
ISBN 0-394-71003-7 (pbk.)

Manufactured in the United States of America
24689753

for and in memory of Janice

Contents

DAYS
and
NIGHTS

In Bed

MORNINGS IN BED

Are energetic mornings.

SNOW IN BED

When we got out of bed
It was snowing.

MEN IN BED

All over Paris
Men are in bed.

BEAUTIFUL GIRL IN BED

Why I am happy to be here.

LONG RELATIONSHIP IN BED

The springs and the bedposts
Are ready the minute we come in.

DOLLS IN BED

With little girls.

HAMMER AND NAILS IN BED

To make it better
They are making it a better bed
And a bigger bed, firmer and larger

And finer bed. So the hammer and nails in the bed
And the carpenter's finger
And thumb and his eyes and his shoulder.
Bang! Bang! Smap! The hammer and nails in bed.

SHEEP IN BED

The sheep got into the bed
By mistake.

BUYING A NEW BED

One of the first things you did
Was buy a new bed.

WINDOW IN BED

I looked at you
And you looked back.

MARRIED IN BED

We'll be married in bed.
The preachers, the witnesses, and all our families
Will also be in bed.

POETRY BED

Whenas in bed
Then, then

OTHER POETRY BED

Shall I compare you to a summer's bed?
You are more beautiful.

4

ORCHIDS IN BED

She placed orchids in the bed
On that dark blue winter morning.

LYING IN BED

Bed with Spain in it
Bed with Gibraltar in it
Bed of art!

LOVERS IN BED

Are lovers no more
Than lovers on the street.
(See Picasso's "Pair of Young Mountebanks," FC 533,
Greuze's "Noces," or hear Mozart's "Fleichtscausenmusik,"
    Köchel 427)

SOME BED

Once
Held
This
All

GOD IN BED

Christ
Was not
Born
(And did
Not die)
In a bed.

LÉGER IN BED

Above our apartment
In 1955
Lived Fernand Léger.

SHOUTING IN BED

We wake up
To the sound of shouts.

FRIENDS IN BED

Sleep well.

ANGELIC CEREMONY IN BED

Putting on the sheets.

MYSTERY OF BED

She takes it for granted
That he will stay up all night long.

WORKMEN IN BED

With workmen's wives
And workmen's girl friends
And other workmen
And dolls.

ACAPULCO IN BED

In Mexico, with blue shimmering water,
Acapulco is in bed.

MY INTOXICATION IN BED

Was not long-lasting.
Was fantastic.
Did not lead me to be very well-mannered.
Wasn't completely romantic.

BASKETBALL IN BED

The basketball is thrown on the bed.

EXPENSIVE BED

At the Lutétia 500 francs a night
In the Hôpital St-Antoine 1000 francs a night

THEATRICAL BED

Exceeded expectations
And received applause.

SIRENS IN BED

My face is plastered to the window
When the sirens come.

COURTSHIP IN BED

"Please. Tell me you like me."
"How did you get in this bed?"

WET DOG IN BED

There is nothing like a wet dog in bed.

DOG BED

In the dog bed
I cannot sleep.

ATOMIC BED

Billions of—uncountable—electrons
Compose this bed.

BEING IN BED

Belongs to everyone
Bed with Spain in it
Bed of art!

SNOW IN BED (LATER)

When it stopped snowing
We still hadn't gone to bed

PHILOSOPHY IN BED

(I)
Plato says this bed
Isn't the real one.
What did Plato know
About beds?

(II)
Spinoza constructed a bed
Which was slept in by Alfred North Whitehead.

(XLIV)
You say, "Let's go to bed"
But those words have no meaning.

8

SOUTH AMERICA IN BED

Brazil, Argentina, Ecuador, and Peru
Are in bed. The first thing you did
Was to buy a new bed.

AS WE LAY IN BED

We saw the stars starting to come together
As we lay in bed.

POLIZIANO IN BED

Angelo Poliziano
Never went to bed
Was it he or Castiglione—
The perfect Renaissance man?

LUNCH IN BED

It's late! Get up! The roseate fruit trees
Are blushing with the nape of new-frocked day!
Awake! The modern breeze of spring
Is pulsative through nest-caroming branches!

COWARDS IN BED

Afraid to turn over. Come on. Come on, turn over.
  Cowards in bed.

CHOPIN'S ÉTUDES IN BED

Here is the bed
Of Chopin's Études;
Over here is his Préludes' bed;
And here is the bed of his Mazurkas.

PRÉLUDES IN BED

There are no préludes in bed
Today.

LET'S GO TO BED

When the tree
Is blossoming. It will be
A long time
Before it is blossoming again.

STONES IN BED

In the bed are stones
From Egypt and Etruria
And some magazines and a pouch of tobacco.

BED

I'd wake up every morning
And look out the window across the park.

WOODEN MECHANICAL FIGURE INDICATING A BED

With a mighty smile
And a mighty gesture
He discloses the bed.

Y. SICK IN BED

Said, If there is a heaven
I want it to look
Like what is out there.

MORNINGS IN BED

Are pensive mornings.

SUICIDE

I was unable to tell you any reason
To get out of bed

A BLUE AND WHITE BED

Became a yellow and gold one,
Then was green, pale green,
Then violet, then onyx,
Yes onyx, then it was an onyx bed.

BALCONIES IN BED

When you lean over
When you fall
When you speak

BEDS IN THE GARDENS OF SPAIN

To the sound of a guitar
When you enter the room.

POETRY IN BED

Do you remember how this started—
With "Mornings in Bed" and "Snow in Bed"?

RISPETTO

Good-bye to bed.
The ceiling loses its chance
To see you smile again
In just that way.

LUXEMBOURG BED

The bed flies past
Like a swing.

ADVANCE BED

Advance arm. Advance stairs. Advance power.
Advance bed.

CHILD BED

You had two babies
Before we met.

ABSTRACT BED

There is paint
On the abstract bed.

ORCHIDS IN BED

She placed orchids on the bed
On a dark red winter afternoon.

12

AT ENDEBED

At Endebed I mett you
You go up on the lift, no, yes
Then we hearing from sounds of guitars
Americans strolling bingo hatrack in the lake.

ENEMIES IN BED

Enemies sleep in separate beds
But in the same part of the city.

PRIMAVERA

He makes up the bed
And follows her home.

ESTATE

The bed lies in the room
The way she lies in the bed.

SAWBED

In the bed of the saw
The sawdust is dying.

WINDOWBED

From henna to blue all violet is in bed.

ZEN BED

I can't get to bed.
Show me the bed and I will show you how to get to it.

LARGE SUNDAY BED

Domingo.
Domenica.
Dimanche.

SATURDAY BED

Sabato.

SNOW IN BED

When we get out of bed
There is no more bed.

WOMEN IN BED

Everywhere in Paris
Women are in bed.

MARRIED IN BED

We did not get married
In bed.

FALSE BED
There are Easter eggs
Red blue yellow and white-pink
In the false bed.

INVITING SOMEONE FROM BED

Come, let me help you out of bed.
The sun is shining. The window is open. Look!
From the balcony there is the street, which is like a bed.

THE FUTURE BED

Will be lilac in color
And in the shape of an L or a Z.

GUITARS IN BED

When we get out of bed
We hear guitars.

POST-MODERNISM IN BED

Kandinsky, Arp, Valéry, Léger, and Marinetti
Are kicked out of bed.
Then, for a long time, nobody gets back into it.

THE HOLIDAYS OF BED

Are when no one is there.

GEORGICS IN BED

Planting wheat and rye and oats—explaining how to do it
And when, what kind of sunlight is needed and how much
    rain.

STRANGE BEDFELLOWS

The bear got into bed
With his claws.

CHAIRMAN BED

There is a little red book
In the bed.

SHOWER BED

For her engagement they gave her a shower
And for her marriage they went to bed.

MANTEQUILLA BED

Butter bed, beurre bed, burro bed.

THESMOPHORIAZUSAE IN BED

Euripides put the Thesmophoriazusae in bed;
Then he also put in bed Elektra, Jason, and Sophocles.
Aristophanes said, Here, let me put you to bed.
No! Euripides screamed. But Aristophanes did
Put Euripides into bed with the Thesmophoriazusae.

POETRY BED

To have it all at once, and make no decisions.
But that is a decision.

OLIVE TREE BED

Along the side of the hill
Amid the green and gray trees
There is a place that looks like a bed.

I AM SORRY I DIDN'T EXPECT TO FIND YOU IN BED

With me I must have misdialed the telephone oh
Wait a minute—damn! I can't extricate
Myself from these sheets yes I'm getting up what
Did you expect after such a long night at the factory
Of unexplained phenomena with your head and shoulders
Beautiful as a telephone directory but please don't talk to
    me about love

16

I have an appointment with my head with the dead with a
    pheasant
With a song I'm nervous good-bye. It was the end of bed.

STREAM BED

In the stream bed
The snails go to sleep.

PHILOSOPHY OF BED

A man should be like a woman and a woman should be like
    an animal
In bed is one theory. Another is that they both should be
    like beds.

WE NEVER WENT TO BED

Listen, Kenny, I think it's a great idea! said Maxine
And she helped me sell my book to Chelsea House.
It was spring, with just the slightest hint of white and pink
    in the branches.

MALLARMÉ'S BED

An angel came, while Mallarmé lay in bed,
When he was a child, and opened its hands
To let white bouquets of perfumed stars snow down.

PSYCHOANALYTIC CRITICISM IN BED

What are you trying to avoid talking about
When you talk about bed?

STORM IN BED

It was such a bad storm
That we were hurled out of bed.

FLEURUS BED

There were flowers on the wallpaper,
There was loss and present excitement,
There was hope for the future, anxiety about the past,
Doubts and hopes about my work, and much to come,
As I lay in my bed on the rue de Fleurus.

CARTOON BED

The door swings open and the bed comes in
Making a tremendous racket and bumping around.

OWL IN BED

The owl flew into bed
By mistake.

DAY BED

When I loved you
Then that whole time
Was like a bed
And that whole year
Was like a day bed.

DENIED BED

We were not in bed
When summer came.

LE FORÇAT DU MOULIN À GAZ IN BED

The convict of the gas mill is in bed.

SNOW IN BED

Vanishing snowflakes, rooftops appearing
And sidewalks and people and cars as we get out of bed.

DISCOBOLUS IN BED

The discus thrower
Is still in bed.

The World

Sic transit ego
And sic fugit this poem
I'm through with it
A little yellow-stomached bird
Just leaped on my porch board.
I need to figure out
What is going on.
If bird so happy
And I so unhappy
I'm not in concordance with the world.

Once all contained
In me and around
Waterfall ahead
Whirlpool ahead
Rapids ahead
Poetic fame ahead
Dog ahead dawn ahead
Being less comic ahead
Fortune ahead misfortune ahead
Old age ahead and death ahead
Everything ahead
Inside my heart ahead and in my brain ahead
Meeting her ahead having met you ahead
And ahead even ahead
And within me contained
It bores and depresses me
It excites me
When I finish the day is gone

Everything still ahead
No longer can I believe
For me or a part of me
No one will be surprised

Saying I ought to see
Suffering is simply that
A thing for every day.
Can one person cure me?
Am I sick? I am
Unhappy and I think
I shouldn't be.

Whist! where are you gone, bird?
Departed without a word
Naturally.
Have I won
My freedom to damn myself
To my enemy's exclusive company?
Poetry, my enemy!
Why can't you do everything?
Make me young again.
Give me that hand in my hand.

Girl and Baby Florist Sidewalk
Pram Nineteen Seventy Something

Sweeping past the florist's came the baby and the girl
I am the girl! I am the baby!
I am the florist who is filled with mood!
I am the mood. I am the girl who is inside the baby
For it is a baby girl. I am old style of life. I am the new
Everything as well. I am the evening in which you docked
    your first kiss.
And it came to the baby. And I am the boyhood of the girl
Which she never has. I am the florist's unknown baby
He hasn't had one yet. The florist is in a whirl
So much excitement, section, outside his shop
Or hers. Who is he? Where goes the baby? She
Is immensely going to grow up. How much
Does this rent for? It's more than a penny. It's more
Than a million cents. My dear, it is life itself. Roses?
Chrysanthemums? If you can't buy them I'll give
Them for nothing. Oh no, I can't.
Maybe my baby is allergic to their spores.
So then the girl and her baby go away. Florist stands
    whistling
Neither inside nor outside thinking about the mountains of
    Peru.

With Janice

The leaves were already on the trees, the fruit blossoms
White and not ruined and pink and not ruined and we
Were riding in a boat over the water in which there was a
    sea
Hiding the meanings of all our salty words. A duck
Or a goose and a boat and a stone and a stone cliff. The
Hardnesses—and, with a little smile—of life. Sitting
Earlier or later and forgotten the words and the bees
At supper they were about in how you almost gestured but
    stopped
Knowing there were only one or two things, and that the
    rest
Were merely complications. But one in a trenchcoat said
It's reversible. And, It's as out-of-date as a reversible coat.
    And
Magna Bear and Minor Orse were sleeping. The soap
Was climbing in its dish but relaxed and came down when
    cold water stopped
Rushing in and the bathroom was flooded. I said, It is not
    about
Things but with things I'd like to go and, too, Will it last
Or will all become uniform again? Even as she goes
Pottering around the island's peripheries she thinks
Of the obligations. And the sympathies, far stronger than
    bears.
I was a bush there, a hat on a clothes dummy's head.
    Receiving letters
Sat down. I avoided being punished. I said,
It's cutting the limbs off a tree but there was no
Tree and I had no saw. I was planning to have infinite
    egress
While keeping some factory on the surface exceedingly
    cold. It was

A good source of evening. Sweating, asleep in the after-
Noons, later the morning of thumps, unwhittled questions,
    the freezing head. At night
Drinking whiskey, the fishermen were, everyone said, away.
A chrysanthemum though still full of splashes it
Has lost some little of its odor for my nostrils and a girl
In a chalk-pink-and-white dress is handing on the cliff
A glass of emerald water to a pin, or is it a chicken, as you
    get
Closer you can see it is a mirror made of the brawn
Of water muscles splashing that which has been.
My self, like the connections of an engine—rabbits and the
    new year—
Having puzzled out something in common, a blue stone
    duck
As if Homer Hesiod and Shakespeare had never lived at all
And we weren't the deposit. Weinstein puts on his hat
And the women go crazy. Some falter toward the sea.
    Wein-
Stein come back! But he is leaving. He says Leonard!
    Good-bye!
So Leonard invites us
To come and to see, where the white water bucket is a
    dashboard
Of this place to that. You will want to go swimming, and
    you will want to meet
These snobbish absurd Americans who inhabit
The gesso incalcations on the cliff. And we went like a nose
To a neighbor face. Sometimes tilting the grappa
Or in this case the ouzo it spills on my clothes or on yours,
    the world without us, the world outside
As when one of us was sick, which also brought the out
    world in.
And the art world meanwhile
Was strumming along. Individual struggles
Will long be remembered, of XXX's doing this,
Of YYYY's doing that.

Soap which will start lazily up from those types. Then
We remember to leave and also to stay. Janice said
It may not be hooked on right. Weinstein has been walking
Down a flowery way. Good-bye, nature lovers! he
  crescendoed.
A locked sail. The bullet of this button isn't right. And the
  train laughed
And pulled out pulling half of the station with it. The dust
Was indifferent to Americans as to Greeks. What simply
  was happening
Was beyond the rustication of ideas into the elements but
  essentially the same. Meanwhile, grasses matted,
The leaves winced, ideas one had had in earliest childhood
  days
Were surprisingly becoming succinct, maybe just before
  vanishing
Or turning into something you would feel like a belt,
Circling but not in hand. I would find these and set them
  down
On the sizzling white paper that was slipperier than the
  knees
That made me feel guilty, and sometimes heavier than the
  overcoats which there we never had
For someone's chest's attention. It was always distraction
But it was also a chair. And a chair is merely a civilized
  distraction. If
Character wasn't everything, it was something else I didn't
Know less than geography, which is to say, Surprise,
  Wonder,
Delight. You stood there and the stones
Of Old Greece and our lives, those collegiate stones,
Harvard, Emory, and Marymount, with the blue exegesis of
  the tide
Against which to fall was a headline—Don't stand.
You give this wish to me—Apollo, in some manner of time,
  lives on. Inside your mind
Things are being washed. Everything was docking

And we went down to see it. Memories of women made
  exactly the same
Kneeling down in the hot raft of daisies
It also got ragged for my walks. When are we going
To really have the time to have time? I make love to you
Like a rope swinging across a stone wall and you
Are lilacs reflected in a mirror or seen through a window.
Going out. You said I like this one. A pale pink dress
The suds were driving through the water. Moving fairly fast
  against the
Just plain oxygen we ended up looking
A little bit overcome. But I got up
You got up. We went around
Spilling things and putting a few of them on racks.
Those were the important things we never got done
Because they were behind us or
Surpassing us, otherwise unavailable—cherry
Blossoms, clavicles of girls which I can't touch
In the innocuousness, beetles, burring and scampering
  around a rose
I see is no longer there. Blossoms on the walk we were
  here, were there
As much as the heat was. I dried my ear at the sink
Then dried the other and quieted my lips and my nose
With a briny dry towel and you slid upon your shoes
And Katherine jumped up, ran around. Soon she will be
Out as usual, down the roadway formally unopened
For my approach, as if not to be drunk
Were a confidence vote from the leaves for the turmoil
  inside
The ouzo-fed engines of ourselves, when, seated on slabs of
  wood
As roses on tough ground as eggs were on the morning,
  deciding to leave,
We oversleep the boat, a shirt, a white shirt gleaming
On the photographic exception of the tide. An airlane of
  styles.

If it was said, It's hopeless
And you said, The gardens are going over
The edge of the overside sidewalk. Well,
Maybe and maybe not. A foot, I thought (not very
    intelligently)
In a shoe of newspapers, even ice unstacked about by
    process—
I loved the texture of your talk, and another woman's
Breast had a texture of a late summer day, while your
Eyes were walking both inside your head and in me, in
    each of my activities
While you both found the cat and he was seated, alive,
Beyond ants, on some anthill pebbles and or gravel. The
    bar wasn't closed
Or open, it was daylight-surprised. Plate glass was nowhere
    around.
I looked up. I put on my glasses. There were all these
    artists
Hot with the prayers of nineteen sixty-one—
Let us be potters, or skunks, but not
Business men! I sat down on a stone
And looked around, my last chance
To never be a doctor, as if it meant something, and a
    father of four—
In these minutes, of fatal decisions. Decisions! Fatal! Lazy,
Air comes in. What could it have been
To be so exciting? And the Scotch tape jumped into the air
With Leonardo out in a boat, and, miles later, acropoles of
    bones the dead
Dinosaurs and cities, tied to subjects
All of us present have forgotten—women, failing the
    Weinstein
Of the season. Rather inform
P.M. while you are re-estimating buttons'
Life by leaving them long-ungone-for in the midst
Of the very short walks we take down the long
Bite narrow street—At night electricity is kissing

The emasculated stars—The new things we had done, in
    pencil at the side of the napkin.
It was hot. Ce qui veut dire we, a cat sitting
On a balcony a plant was wilting. What dialect are you
    speaking,
You, wearing the loafers of the sea? I couldn't care
For everything simultaneously. A mat was exciting enough.
    The bath came separately
From the dawn. You walk around
Simply looking for strawberries, sun, our baby, oxygen—
"Always not quite unbeginning to be or have been begun."
Leonardo erat other. Iras haec perturbat. Let that be.
    Another was
Absent in a habit fidget. I was
In a rush. Someone said, hush!
Calm down in this—knife—patterns of things—
Where is the music that's fitting for such an occasion
In those miles of hotel
Corridor followed by Weinstein's weeping at the beach
Girls who followed that for love of him
And why is there not more peaceful melting here
Into the wide wood story of the wall
How I loved those made of stone. And yet poetry has
Messages, interrogations of musics that have been used
In the various islands of acts, staying genuinely still,
And seeing—a piece of life and seeing—
It's a wall inside me
Why dancers were always coming out in a pageant
Wrecking the place animals were in there too
As now, so for music fit?
The pink spot you trotted me out to see with under the
    sigh which
Something and the great writers were all still alive
Much of the worst had happened, the envelope was still
    unpeeled.
I am stamping on the path. Alone. Nothing is so essential
    as this—

Moment. And a red fan wings past—flower? Transatlantic
   systems ourselves
The door unopened, the mail came every day. The grass is
   soft,
Matted, and then there was an enclosure, tar on my leg, on
   yours
The culture all around us was in fragments, in some chests
   sure
In others fragments, in some no grasp at all, which I
   couldn't
Easily perceive, thus making everybody equal,
Almost at least enough to be a rival—perception,
Inspiration—too cloud to care. Voices
I heard on rooftops and cul-de-sacs of meditative sex
Scurried beyond the invisible barrier of you washing
The blouse. Brilliant. In fact, having more meaning
Because of all impulsions. You were
A blue coat—it wasn't
Exactly yours or mine or that place's
But a stinginess of life in packet flying through
Eventually, signing away like papers
A moment of the beach, when the tide dried the invincible
By elbows in comparison to the nude inside—
Look at—it's finished; this rock
Will come with me! Weinstein, walking in his sleep
The first afternoon when I arrived cooling bees they have a
   hive
Against the cliff, who've kept things in—the art
School, slacks. Normal the Mediterranean
Flows onward and on, boat,
I wore Leonard's jacket and my clothes, then shoes
Meet yours, advancing, so walk about the best
Final of beach, to not notice numbers
Except when they are speaking, as we stopped less
When all this was around.

Twenty Poems

1

The diary is open at two o'clock.
Words of love are in it! Words of passion and of love!

2

HEROIC STANDARD

The street winds slowly through the meadow
Where a city once was. Thousands of bluets crawl to cover
   it
But the street winds on.

3

1958

The violets in the tempest withered, shrunk.
The toilet flushed. The air came liberally in the windows.
Workers went on strike. Somebody else was crazed by
   somebody else.

4

At the fish market we walked back and forth.
You were thinner. My doctorate was yet unsought.
I had produced "Variations on William Carlos Williams."
The grammar mistakes were everywhere, I thought.
A view was ours past the clinic.
Someone was starting a shop. Another one, this one,
That one, lived in a château. In Italy that's a palace.
I don't like him. We figured out

30

Everybody running about. Past the streetcar turn-
Around, dark white violets, breakfast, tones
And the roller skates slick on the cement, or tiles.

5

The personality of the feeding bin
The impersonality of the feed
In the stomachs of the birds a flower
Of hunger and of hunger satisfied. Then cold grips the
    street
As my hunger grips the flower of your heart. We eat
Dinner. We go to bed. We wake up. Impenetrable and
    mysterious life!

6

The dawn woke the hats up in Tuscany.
The flares woke the bats up egotistically.
Drinks are finished and songs put down
On tables and now the pianoforte begins.

7

He who addresses you
Turns around a hat
Once, he drinks
Glass after glass of something
Wine. He is not dead. He reminds
You of something else.
That's it! The Assumption.

THE SILENCERS

Eyes coveted your elbows;
Ears cupped against your heart.

ENVIRONMENT

Mist creeps into the environment;
Green is the grass, is the moss, is the whole environment.

Notices are sent up into the music
Telling the music to be silent
While the notes are being read
But the music which is made of notes
Does not understand
And the snow keeps falling.
The concerto goes on, a pandemonium of sound!

DISNEY BOHÈME

The stork A-plus Popeye and Olive Oyl sheep
Footsteps sur la neige Debussy
A warm Paris apartment/living with now dead people
Selling books eating idyllically straight from the pan

ART AND SOCIETY

Formlessness suggested by Debussy's
"Des pas sur la neige"
Copland's repeating the criticism that
Debussy was "bourgeois"
True he wrote in a protected world
No green ate away at his environment
Nor vagrants stormed his windows
None are purple with green rings
In the snow all footsteps are white

AFTER SOME VERSES BY MORVAEN LE GAÉLIQUE AND
    PAUL VERLAINE

Did you call? or was that sound on the telephone
My bad sad beating heart
That only beats for you?
Et puis voici mon corps, not mon coeur,
My body, which is bitten by a barracuda,
And my course, which is straight for you.

Desire and curiosity
Make me feel I'm indestructible.
My actual fragility
Assails me as I write this poem.
And I put the pen down.

15

GORDU WISDOM

An elephant is larger than its master.
The forest is smaller than its trees.

16

Words penetrate a poem
As a dog penetrates a court;
Finding the gateway he wants he sees
His master coming toward him and he barks.

17

TO THE PROSPECT OF TIME

I too remember the summer afternoon
When I was completely happy and alone.

18

AT NIGHT

Nothing can sleep like irony. You say
One thing and you mean another. Oxygen is matrimony's
  brother.
When you sleep, you speak alone.

19

How many things we are attentive to!
Words spoken in sleep, the dog's paw, the emblem-
Atic significance of everything that is done and seen.
Winter, for example, with its damp sleet and boots.

Each moment fills him with a desire
For another moment and each incident he makes
As a result of this situation
Leads to another one and another one and another.
So she might be attracted to
Anyone! It frightens him. He says, She is not like me.
Then he loves her no longer,
For one second.

Days and Nights

It came to me that all this time
There had been no real poetry and that it needed to be
    invented.
Some recommended discovering
What was already there. Others,
Taking a view from further up the hill (remnant
Of old poetry), said just go and start wherever you
    are.

It was not the kind of line
I wanted so I crossed it out
"Today I don't think I'm very inspired"—
What an existence! How hard to concentrate
On what is the best kind of existence!
What's sure is having only one existence
And its already having a shape.

Extase de mes vingt ans—
French girl with pure gold eyes
In which shine internal rhyme and new kinds of stanzas

When I said to F, Why do you write poems?
He said, Look at most of the poems
That have already been written!

All alone writing
And lacking self-confidence
And in another way filled with self-confidence
And in another way devoted to the brick wall
As a flower is when hummed on by a bee

I thought This is the one I am supposed to like best
The totally indifferent one
Who simply loves and identifies himself with something
Or someone and cares not what others think nor of time
The one who identifies himself with a wall.

I didn't think I was crazy
I thought Orpheus chasms trireme hunch coats melody
And then No that isn't good enough

I wrote poems on the edges of the thistles
Which my walking companions couldn't understand
But that's when I was a baby compared to now

"That is so much like you and your poetry."
This puts me in a self-congratulatory mood
Which I want to "feel out," so we sit together and talk
All through the winter afternoon.

I smoked
After writing five or ten lines
To enjoy what I had already written
And to not have to write any more

I stop smoking
Until after lunch
It is morning
It is spring
The day is breaking
Ten—eleven—noon
I am not smoking
I am asleep

Sense of what primitive man is, in cave and with primitive
    life
Comes over me one bright morning as I lie in bed
Whoosh! to the typewriter. Lunch! And I go down.

What have I lost?
The Coleridge joke, as W would say.

William Carlos Williams, I wrote
As the end word of a sestina. And *grass*
Sleepy, hog snout, breath, and *dream.*
I never finished it.

I come down the hill—cloud
I like living on a hill—head
You are so lucky to be alive—jokes
It chimes at every moment—stung

So much of it was beyond me
The winding of the national highway
The fragments of glass in the convent wall
To say nothing of the habits of the bourgeoisie
And all those pleasures, the neat coat,
The bought wine, and the enabling of the pronouncements

For Christ's sake you're missing the whole day
Cried someone and I said Shut up
I want to sleep and what he accomplished in the hours I slept
I do not know and what I accomplished in my sleep
Was absolutely nothing

How much is in the poet and how much in the poem?
You can't get to the one but he gives you the other.
Is he holding back? No, but his experience is like a bubble.
When he gives it to you, it breaks. Those left-over soap
    dots are the work.

Oh you've done plenty I said when he was feeling
    despondent
Look at X and L and M. But they don't do anything, he
    replied.

At the window I could see
What never could be inside me
Since I was twelve: pure being
Without desire for the other, not even for the necktie or
  the dog

The bathtub is white and full of strips
And stripes of red and blue and green and white
Where the painter has taken a bath! Now comes the poet
Wrapped in a huge white towel, with his head full of
  imagery.

Try being really attentive to your life
Instead of to your writing for a change once in a while
Sometimes one day one hour one minute oh I've done that
What happened? I got married and was in a good mood

We wrote so much that we thought it couldn't be any
  good
Till we read it over and then thought how amazing it was!

Athena gave Popeye a Butterfinger filled with stars
Is the kind of poetry Z and I used to stuff in jars

When we took a walk he was afraid
Of the dogs who came in parade
To sniffle at the feet
Of two of the greatest poets of the age.

The stars came out
And I was still writing
My God where's dinner
Here's dinner
My wife! I love you

Do you remember in Paris
When I was thinner
And the sun came through the shutters like a knife

I said to so many people once, "I write poetry."
They said, "Oh, so you are a poet." Or they said,
"What kind of poetry do you write? modern poetry?"
Or "My brother-in-law is a poet also."
Now if I say, "I am the poet Kenneth Koch," they say "I
    think I've heard of you"
Or "I'm sorry but that doesn't ring a bell" or
"Would you please move out of the way? You're blocking
    my view
Of that enormous piece of meat that they are lowering into
    the Bay
Of Pigs." What? Or "What kind of poetry do you write?"

"Taste," I said to J and he said
"What else is there?" but he was looking around.

"All the same, she isn't made like that,"
Marguerite said, upon meeting Janice,
To her husband Eddie, and since
Janice was pregnant this had a clear meaning
Like the poetry of Robert Burns.

You must learn to write in form first, said the dumb poet.
After several years of that you can write in free verse.
But of course no verse is really "free," said the dumb poet.
Thank you, I said. It's been great talking to you!

Sweet are the uses of adversity
Became Sweetheart cabooses of diversity
And Sweet art cow papooses at the university
And sea bar Calpurnia flower havens' re-noosed knees

A book came out, and then another book
Which was unlike the first,
Which was unlike the love
And the nightmares and the fisticuffs that inspired it
And the other poets, with their egos and their works,
Which I sometimes read reluctantly and sometimes with
   great delight
When I was writing so much myself
I wasn't afraid that what they wrote would bother me
And might even give me ideas.

I walked through the spring fountain of spring
Air fountain knowing finally that poetry was everything:
Sleep, silence, darkness, cool white air, and language

3. THE SECRET

Flaming
They seem
To come, sometimes,
Flaming
Despite all the old
Familiar effects
And despite my knowing
That, well, really they're not flaming
And these flaming words
Are sometimes the best ones I write
And sometimes not.

The doctor told X don't write poetry
It will kill you, which is a very late example
Of the idea of the immortal killing the man
(Not since Hector or one of those people practically)
X either wrote or didn't I don't remember—
I was writing (what made me think of it)
And my heart beat so fast
I actually thought I would die.

Our idea is something we talked about, our idea
Our idea is to write poetry that is better than poetry
To be as good as or better than the best old poetry
To evade, avoid all the mistakes of bad modern poets
Our idea is to do something with language
That has never been done before
Obviously—otherwise it wouldn't be creation
We stick to it and now I am a little nostalgic
For our idea, we never speak of it any more, it's been
Absorbed into our work, and even our friendship
Is an old, rather fragile-looking thing.
Maybe poetry took the life out of both of them,
Idea and friendship.

I like the new stuff you're doing
She wrote and then she quoted some lines
And made some funny references to the poems
And he said have you forgotten how to write the other
    kind of poems
Or, rather, she said it I forget which
I was as inspired as I have ever been
Writing half-conscious and half-unconscious every day
After taking a walk or looking at the garden
Or making love to you (as we used to say)

Unconscious meant "grace"
It meant No matter who I am
I am greater than I am
And this is greater
And this, since I am merely the vessel of it,
May be the truth

Then I read Ariosto
I fell to my knees
And started looking for the pins
I had dropped when I decided to be unconscious

I wanted to fasten everything together
As he did and make an enormous poetry Rose
Which included everything
And which couldn't be composed by the "unconscious"
(At least not by the "unconscious" alone)

This rose became a bandanna, which became a house
Which became infused with all passion, which became a
    hideaway
Which became yes I would like to have dinner, which
    became hands
Which became lands, shores, beaches, natives on the stones
Staring and wild beasts in the trees, chasing the hats of
Lost hunters, and all this deserves a tone
That I try to give it by writing as fast as I can
And as steadily, pausing only to eat, sleep, and as we used
    to say, make love
And take long walks, where I would sometimes encounter a
    sheep
Which gave me rhyming material and often a flowering
    fruit tree,
Pear apple cherry blossom thing and see long paths winding
Up hills and then down to somewhere invisible again
Which I would imagine was a town, in which another
    scene of the poem could take place.

4. OUT AND IN

City of eternal flowers
And A said Why not make it paternal flowers
And Z said Or sempiternal There were bananas
Lying on the closet shelf by the couch
Forty feet from where your miscarriage began
And we were talking about this nonsense
Which meant so much to us, meant so much to us at the time.

Ponte Vecchio going over the Arno
What an image you are this morning
In the eye of almighty God!
I am the old bridge he said she said
I forget if it was a boy or a girl
A sexless thing in my life
Like sidewalks couches and lunch

Walking around nervously then going in the house
The entire problem is to sit down
And start writing. Solved! Now the problem
Is to get up. Solved! Now the problem
Is to find something equally worthwhile to do. Solved!
Thank you for coming to see me. But
Thank you for living with me. And
Thank you for marrying me. While
Thank you for the arguments and the fights
And the deadly interpellations about the meanings of
    things!

Your blue eyes are filled with storms
To alter and mildly disarrange an image of someone's, he
    said it about the eyelid
But you are crying. I have a pain in my side.

The idea of Mallarmé
That
Well that it was so
Vital
Poetry, whatever it was
Is inspiring
Is I find even more inspiring
Than his more famous idea
Of absence
And his famous idea
Of an uncertain relationship of the words
In a line to make it memorably *fugace.*

Absence and I were often in my room
Composing. When I came out you and absence were
  wielding a broom
Which was a task I hadn't thought of in my absence
Finally absence took over
You, me, the broom, my writing, my typewriter,
Florence, the house, Katherine, everything.

Well, I don't know—those were great moments
Sometimes and terrible moments sometimes
And sometimes we went to the opera
And sometime later the automobile squeaked
There is no such thing as an automobile, there is only a
  Mercedes or a Ferrari
Or a Renault Deux Chevaux is that a Citroën
There is What do we care what kind of car but
Often in the sunshine we did. That's
When we were traveling I wasn't writing.

You've got to sit down and write. Solved!
But what I write isn't any good. Unsolved!
Try harder. Solved! No results. Unsolved!
Try taking a walk. Solved! An intelligent, pliable,
Luminous, spurting, quiet, delicate, amiable, slender
  line
Like someone who really loves me
For one second. What a life! (Solved!) Temporarily.

What do you think I should do
With all these old poems
That I am never going to even look at again
Or think about or revise—Throw them out!
But if I raise my hand to do this I feel like Abraham!
And no sheep's around there to prevent me.
So I take another look.

We asked the bad poet to come and dine
The bad poet said he didn't have time
The good poet came and acted stupid
He went to sleep on the couch
But grandiose inspiration had arrived for him with the
    wine
Such was the occasion.

Long afternoons, when I'm not too nervous
Or driven, I sit
And talk to the source of my happiness a little bit
Then Baby gets dressed but not in very much it's
Warm out and off we go
For twenty minutes or so and then come back.

Everyone in the neighboring houses
And in the neighboring orchards and fields
Is busily engaged in doing something
(So I imagine) as I sit here and write.

5. DAYS AND NIGHTS

A B C D F I J
L M N R Y and Z were the friends I had who wrote
    poetry
Now A B and C are dead, L N and Y have stopped writing
Z has gotten better than ever and I am in a heavy mood
Wondering how much life and how much writing there
    should be—
For me, have the two become mostly the same?
Mostly! Thank God for the mostly! Last night with you
I felt by that shaken and uplifted
In a way that no writing could ever do.
The body after all is a mountain and words are a mist—
I love the mist. Heaven help me, I also love you.

When the life leaves the body life will still be in the words
But that will be a little and funny kind of life
Not including you on my lap
And looking at me then shading your beautiful eyes.

Do you want me to keep telling
You things about your
Poem or do you want me to stop? Oh
Tell me. What? I don't think
You should have that phrase "burn up" in the first line.
Why not? I don't know. It
Seems a little unlike the rest.

O wonderful silence of animals
It's among you that I best perhaps could write!
Yet one needs readers. Also other people to talk to
To be friends with and to love. To go about with. And
This takes time. And people make noise,
Talking, and playing the piano, and always running around.

Night falls on my desk. It's an unusual situation.
Usually I have stopped work by now. But this time I'm in
    the midst of a thrilling evasion,
Something I promised I wouldn't do—sneaking in a short
    poem
In the midst of my long one. Meanwhile you're patient,
    and the veal's cold.

Fresh spring evening breezes over the plates
We finish eating from and then go out.
Personal life is everything personal life is nothing
Sometimes—click—one just feels isolated from personal
    life
Of course it's not public life I'm comparing it to, that's
    nonsense vanity—
So what's personal life? the old mom-dad-replay joke or

Sex electricity's unlasting phenomenon? That's right. And
   on
This spring evening it seems sensational. Long may it be
   lasting!

It helps me to be writing it helps me to breathe
It helps me to say anything it gives me
I'm afraid more than I give it

I certainly have lost something
My writing makes me aware of it
It isn't life and it isn't youth
I'm still young enough and alive
It's what I wrote in my poems
That I've lost, the way Katherine would walk
As far as the tree line, and how the fruit tree blossoms
Would seem to poke their way into the window
Although they were a long way outside

Yes sex is a great thing I admire it
Sex is like poetry it makes you aware of hands feet arms
   and legs
And your beating heart
I have never been inspired by sex, always by love
And so we talk about "sex" while thinking a little about
   poetry

There are very few poems
Compared to all the thought
And the activity and the sleeping and the falling in love
And out of love and the friendships
And all the talk and the doubts and the excitement
And the reputations and the philosophies
And the opinions about everything and the sensitivity
And the being alone a lot and having to be with others
A lot and the going to bed a lot and getting up a lot and
   seeing

Things all the time in relation to poetry
And so on and thinking about oneself
In this somewhat peculiar way

Well, producing a lot, that's not what
Being a poet is about, said N.
But trying to do so is certainly one of the somethings
It is about, though the products I must say are most
    numinous—
Wisps of smoke! while novels and paintings clouds go
    belching over the way!

Poetry, however, lives forever.
Words—how strange. It must be that in language
There is less competition
Than there is in regular life, where there are always
Beautiful persons being born and growing to adulthood
And ready to love. If great poems were as easy to create as
    people—
I mean if the capacity to do so were as widespread—
Since there's nothing easy about going through a
    pregnancy—
I suppose we could just forget about immortality. Maybe
    we can!

Z said It isn't poetry
And R said It's the greatest thing I ever read
And Y said I'm sick. I want to get up
Out of bed. Then we can talk about poetry
And L said There is some wine
With lunch, if you want some
And N (the bad poet) said
Listen to this. And J said I'm tired and
M said Why don't you go to sleep. We laughed
And the afternoon-evening ended
At the house in bella Firenze.

Cherche-Midi

The boxes
Are attractive there
An animal eats its hay
Now there's a car rental station
Where I used to stand gulping the air
And thinking Fresh paint!
Unpasteurized milk!
The essence is in the small glass on the shelf
The sense is in the line of the nose
And the dark eyes staring
A minuet steps out of your clothes

Inside you a foetus roamed
Above us a pigeon homed
The sun set like a dark star

Uncouth modern church bells
Park bench glistering so
I did it and didn't. The painted leg is gone
Moved down the hall. The quiet stairs are empty.

The problem is
That often, in the morning
It is not yet light
And daily life is gone.
The city is there
And the castle is there, with the stucco
Paintings, and the girl is there
With her painted leg—
If only you—
But already you
And so we seek the impossible

I.e. we look for something hard
To accomplish and in
Its experience we sense an end,
That is, an achievement, and
When I met you on the stairs
You said Ho ho ho you
Weren't part of the problem
I was hastening (hurrying)
Up there so I could write!
Write something, anything,
Can you understand that
Or are you always just
Going up and down the stairs with
That painted white platter on your head?
What a picture
You'd make! Botticelli, Giorgione,
The works. A major endeavor
To collate stucco with wit
And I am frothing
(Figuratively) at the mouth
By now with my verbal
Unstemmingness and the non finire
Of the god-knows-what-is-
Here-and-there-now style.
I was
Singing in the shower one fall day
Mood opened the kitchen
Stripes came out
You're on the stairs
And dead are the moments musicaux
Of the sea, where
My shoe is, about a foot and a half
From the painting. But I am
Thinking about you there
While I am here
When noon starts.

51

Can you, can I
Be satisfied by the masses of time
We're always looking for desire
Like a dime
It's what counts
Your foot mounts
The stair
And walks are everywhere

Walking later
Or sleeping on the floor
This is a pleasure and a confusion
As a camel makes a white vexed swirl
Of the desert sands

The sun is shining
The sum is divine and you are out
I am in; my paper is fine
It proceeds (forward) exceeds (backward)
Until everything is at the same time
False and true
To the invisible
Not giving way
To minor crises of anger and rage
And staying on the boat
Sometimes
Wandering from one hemorrhage
To another of the interview
Often ready to be inquired
Of by some passing desire "Where are you?
And exactly what are you, too?
And in what state of steam is your flesh?"

Strings like stories shine
And past the window flakes of paper
Testimony to live valentine
A gracious start then hand to the chest in pain

And, looking out that window,
I see the boxed window clasped again
By what this series of moments is and is not.

When it shines and is hot, it is cold somewhere,
    Commander.
This envelope, filled with what is not,
Will soon hold a letter.
Inside the letter will be a heart.
I must sit down and write.
Fortune, what does it mean I "must" write?
I think it means nothing.
It is light sorrow experiencing some fleshy tang.
People are hammering murdering plates
To run up and down stairs with, as if
The result were the cause of the bout
With this day of walking in and out
Whether whirled in rage
Or in a sudden wish to be loving or
Conquer something we sit down, brainily,
Breathing, there seem to be only
Two themes (perhaps four or three)
Which engross us really, the
Theme of what I am doing here and
That one of how is this for you

In summer the abstract words
Accompany me to the interview
And till the rickety clickety train
Went slumping past
Accordions I couldn't be sure exactly
What to say "J'ai guéri ta
Petite amie," the doctor said
Galleries are open or closed.
The Dôme is old and sad.
Perhaps it was a mark on an army
Perhaps the broken arm was seriously bleeding

Perhaps I'll stand up
And perhaps you'll come with me
Where Sunday mornings spell
Anxious commerce to our breathing

She is also your daughter
And the smiling inside
The window, that will never be again

And no one wants it to be
Its sad quality is like a color taken from a shelf
Or maybe it isn't. In black and white it is a daylight
Scene. The water flows past
The place where once he or she was.
A mop is flapping against the door
And the street is alone with history.
They eat dinner and close the door
We go out and come in

Related to putting everything off
Related to the gaga mess of sensation
And thought, related to your relations
And to the baggage
Related to death, yours and mine
And everyone else's, the harm that's done,
To heartbeat and to paralysis
Each morning in the sun
Getting (up) out, glad to be alive
Now we have an elevator (ride)
Into the ravenous day
Ravingly beautiful and egregious

As M. said of D.B.
If you can't change it in
The middle—not at all
Family with too much money
Birds with too many wings

I throw the football
And wait for you to sit down
Then you were gone and generous again
And sleep was escaping me
My head knocked otherwise
You came down the stair

Oh tell me what is this history,
Pure, of the foot? Of the curious lance?
Of the apartment vacated by a footfall? Who is that
Sitting in my chair? My self. My son,
August, July, June. He who was never
Born, the mad one, the one crazy over women
And drugs, the one who never saw
Or would know what to do with
A spatula, a losing streak, or a pump, phantom.

Another time it seems
A long time to be new.
And E. said I knew she wasn't, because
She wasn't pretty enough.
I am having trouble
With this time scission. Bump bump.

The roses wear Mercurochrome on their labels
Because they spit at me with thorns.
And S. said, That's very sexy (about a stanza).
I thought, Oh well, happy, thump. It was something
    Christmas
For Thanksgiving, death's-heads for the New Year.
If one was sad, another was plunging into the soul
Of things, wherefrom cometh the truth.

My notepaper suggests to me
A revelation
Weren't those surrealist streetcars leaving their traces

On my cobblestoned mind in a way that I had immediately
    to erase
So you could see them better? Pregnant, and happy, and
    lost.
As if the whole world were contained within you
You are lost in the one outside, like balls and bats.

Only it is quite a lot
To be trying at any one time
The rent was—bang! My
God! I hope you didn't fall down
But it was only the
Typewriter of the sun
Getting too close to the window
As usual unmarked
By anything except the bars
They leave on unmarked windows—in the courtyard
Sunlight

Sleeping on the floor, O Sunday
Mornings of unless-
We-get-it-right!
The sea brought leaves together
And here's a plant—
Now there's an ant
Making its way along that window line
And all is done.

Youthful happiness is done,
With those aesthetic decisions
Earliest muse makes.
You walked out on the hard
Earth surface hard as cement
It was between Christmas and Lent
All our money was spent

You are on the stairs
Carrying a plate
The ant needs a mate
Needs a mate to do what with?
Sometimes it seems
That one place
And another is enough
But then the truth starts
Don't want to die don't want to lose
What dying constantly renews
One small round era of the eye

In other days, in other lives
The sense of this one?

Astonished giants spark the ocean's side
Alone there for fifty years

When you were at the interview
These monuments are minutes because they are alive
A seagull flies toward them, that is my mind, then goes
    away
You had to figure out which one was me
And try to be nice to it. Hello there!

Like a hammer that's been covered with hay
Like breath, like breasts
Like clams opening and closing themselves
Like always looking for what you always never knew
Could be in taking off your shoes when you were
    alive
And writing, though it never became less blue
Or more so than one morning in Paris
When I was looking out the window
That moment had no importance at all

Such diffidence!
It's made of lead.

It mixes adventure with self-protection
We dressed up to go to the plays
Japanese drama which is so far from my intention
Seemingly legs
Legs in the morning and legs at night
As if all the between times of day
Were not spent I say
With this frenetic happiness true
To whatever arises in you

They walk and are running
A pretty girl made them run over borders
Of cement until where she had given orders
She could be expected and when not there
Was replaced by the loneliness recreation
Of what I could not expect, just air and
Expectation outside there, still walking around a
    lot
With thinking I am nothing but
Repository of these sensations
Which yet are not what I'm about
To say to the stairs
A moving theme, and the reflection
Of the bourgeois tractor going past.

The problem in the morning
Is knowing this and that
And what is the day supposed to do with that?

I establish five things in the interview
Our apartment is like a hat
The elevator goes up and down
Now there are only stairs

Stark white lights over sleephood—
To compose
To veritably verily veritably compose

In B flat
In you, English Language, like a storm

Tossing against the wall
So suddenly! restlessly! and when awake
I was shooting the rent gap
By writing
But not crap
The good English language of the walls
Oh the sidewalks they are simply the bugs' walls
Sideways in action

We expect to live seventy years
Even eighty, ninety, or more
Pour quoi faire? On the stroke
Of eight o'clock to say It's here
The dinner is served in the alcove! while expediting
I am waiting
I walk around
While the hammer hits
With a pie-plate sound
(Come to the interview!)
On whitest sidewalks
(And try that trill again)
Inside me is something that is cold
And starry and outside
Are you, restoration and score
I'll take this necklace yes
And bracelet bone
Good morning, streets
Red is a diamond
Red is more than a color

As the Communist poets say, though
I don't mean it that way
This crocus morning.

Go in. Gratifying.
Nothing happens. Can I speak
To the person I am supposed to interview?
"I'm not at home"—
Like people on the rivers
Dreaming of the strong breasts and the happiness of
    scissors

When I look at the window
Just beyond it, there, across the street
This is how they live it, one foot
On the floor, then, head on the table, then
Other foot high
On the stairs

Street under plate and the sound
Of all that has gone on
In the evening, morning, to sit down
Passing it off as eternity, when really—

The roof shows
How the rain feels

Good morning, spendthrift
Or is that only a butterfly
I wouldn't mind
I wood end mine ud
Together we're free as a cow
When I write two legs are displaced

I am up at eight thirty
And ringing a doorbell at ten
Can you see me? We agreed

Oh I know but—that baby's smile again
And the woman at the window
Out on the balcony she steps
Hair blows in the wind
Cutting the earth in two
With a memory: daily life—silent—and the sun
That is falling today

The Green Step

1/ The Green Step

The green step was near the two girls, five-year-olds, in white rather stiff dresses cut out of lace the way valentines sometimes used to be, and they gesticulated toward it, little fingers pointing this way and that. A bird landed twenty feet away from it. The green step was cold and alone. This step had green carpeting on it which had once been mold, a sort of wet tough tissue of mashed-down grass, stems and leaves—"step mulch." At some time this had changed to a carpet. This carpet was much the same color as the mold of green, though less cold to touch, and with a different smell, not dank and brackish but slightly musty, with a suggestion of chalk or of glue. Underneath this covering, the step was gray-white stone. The step led to the front door of a house. It also led to a small auditorium's stage. It led, once, to a place where a throne began. It led to a place where there is a statue surrounded—on all sides, at a distance of five feet—by columns. The statue is of Diana, the goddess of the chase and of the moon. The white columns around this goddess who so affected the inside and the outside of the woods are not much like trees, although they are tall, straight up, and sometimes cold, and one could hide behind them, hide behind one of them if one were small and slim enough. And this, one of the little girls once did. That was before the step led to a concert stage or into a house. The place with the columns seemed, though no one knew why, to have been the first place to which the step went.

Standing on the step one felt between one place and another. Those who went to see the statue of Diana, those who went to the concert or into the house, had never met the man who made the step. The step was originally a random step in the woods. It led a wild life, not wild in itself but lying amidst nature, and being part of it, in random arrangements. A very

long time ago the arrangement had been changed by an earth-
quake; more recently, by a man. That was the man who made
the step. He took pleasure in finding the stone, in carrying it
away with him. The next day he made the step. The bird flew
some distance away.

That was only one time the step was made. At other times
it was changed and became different steps. What happened to
the step at one time or another did not very much affect the
main characteristic, for most of those who used it or even those
who saw it, of the step. Its main quality was that it was solid,
it could be relied on, it would take you from one place to the
next. Oh, people had fallen off the step, but that was never due
to any fault of the step. They fell because they were ill, suddenly, or because they had drunk too much alcohol, or even,
sometimes, because they were pushed. Not everyone who came
up on the step was welcome at all times to whoever happened
to be at the top of the step, or rather where the step led to.
However the step is not very high, and no one has been seriously hurt from falling when he was standing on it.

The step had no consciousness of the change in its existence
from being amidst wild nature to being a part of something
that an animate and mobile species had turned into an object
which served one of its manifold purposes. The step had, in
fact, no consciousness of a world at all. Children would look
at the step, sometimes, and think it felt something, but there
is no evidence that it did. The step was there, and one day
someone stepped on it who killed the bird.

The house the step leads to is a large house with bedrooms
upstairs, and a large living room and dining room downstairs
and a modern kitchen. It was built a long time ago but the
family who own it live somewhere else and the house is rented
to a father, a mother, and a son. The son is a hunter. The father
spends his days placing cards in a long rectangular cardboard
box. The mother goes into different rooms of the house and
her clothing almost always has pleats. The member of the
family who spends the most time on the step is the son. He

will stand there leaning and looking out at the life of man and nature beyond the house. A domestic servant will sometimes stand there, too, replacing the boy.

The stone that forms the basis of the step, under the green carpeting, is slightly veined with grayish white in a way that suggests distances. The lines move outward and suggest a beyond that no one in the story is able to get to. The stone is thought to be made up of rapidly moving electrons, though this is not part of the common experience of anyone who sees it.

The step in the concert hall is the step that goes to the house and that goes to the throne. The throne is made of majolica, silver, and amber. No one is sitting on the throne. No one is playing in the concert hall. The house is rotting, empty, and is being destroyed. The sound of bulldozers, the noise of drilling things fills the street. There is dust everywhere around, making one passer-by think "I would like to get out of all this; I'll go to a concert." The man with a blue hat says, "It is foolish to waste this step." The step is taken to, and sold for a very small sum to the man who arranges performances in the concert hall. Before, leading to the stage, he had only a rotting wooden step. It's a strange thing to buy, he thinks, a step, but yes, I guess I can use it. Now there is an irregular noise—tuning up of instruments. When the concert is over, the people go out into the street. In the air, for a moment, are their comments on what they have heard.

Now night invests the street, and the step leads to a throne. High above the buildings and the trees, azure, blood- and sulphur-colored formations move about the sky. On her head appear three stars for a crown. Her feet, like clouds, are white. Thundering over the universe, the rainstorm washes this away. Washes her away.

When someone speaks of the step, which had once been part of the house, another says that then there was no green carpet on the step. That would only have been when the step was inside a building. Now in the concert hall, yes, there is green carpeting covering the step, but not before. It is even possible to argue, lightly, as to whether or not it is the same step.

Ideally the step would be part of the procurement of some sort of final fulfillment for everyone, and perhaps it is. The woman knows she will have to sell the piano. She sits down to play it, and once again the child starts to cry. The old man looks at the step and remembers the bird. Every day, for a week, as a child, he had seen it. The concert hall seems to become for him a sort of temple with yellow and white mists beyond, and green and vermilion stripes among its columns, and where one who is a statue, in a final wash of violets and whites, leans over to him and plants a stony kiss on his trembling face. Ah! he screams aloud and everyone turns to look at him. They do not see what is the matter. He walks in the woods. Every day is like a light kiss given by the country, by its air, by its sun, by its trees. There still seems to be no reason to think of a king or a god. Feet tread on the step and the trigger is released. Birds fly in a dance of blood-splatters all over the wall—a painting much later than Cézanne. In the morning the step is nothing and no one in anyone's thoughts. Contracts are made at the Bourse and on the real estate tables. Flies buzz hopelessly against the windows. Men in shirtsleeves, in billows of cigarette smoke, say, "We must take the first step." A dog jumps up, its paws against a little girl's white dress. Her mother is miles away, in a car. The old man is here. A servant comes down the step and picks the child up.

2/ The Brook

The blue, fluffy bird lands on a gray stone and looks around him. Who knows if he hears the white-blue brook that is going by? He certainly hears, smells or feels something, because, perched on this stone, he dips his beak once, twice, three times in the bubbly stream. This brook starts in the mountains— well, really they are just tall hills, which, in back of the houses, rise toward the once-supposed geographical location of heaven, which is now thought either to be a myth, or, if it does represent something really existing, then to be something that can be found in our own bodies, thoughts, and hearts. About the brook, sitting on the ground, was a rather varied group of people: a young girl from India, in a sari, with a spot of blue paint or some kind of cosmetic, on her forehead, named Shara; a boy from the United States, with a great mop of hair; a young Frenchman whose heart was even now beating only faintly, and who, unbeknownst to himself and everyone else there, would soon be dead; and a French girl, about seventeen, with a rather wide forehead, blue eyes, and a dreamy smile. Her name was Hélène. The men's names were not as important as the girls' names. They had not yet come, for anyone there, to represent high states of abstraction for things beautiful and loved.

The bird, suddenly aware of the people, flies off. The French girl looks at the bird. "How beautiful it is!" "Comme il est beau!" The young Frenchman's gravestone is five miles away, two miles from the nearest point of the brook. The Indian girl pushes her sari lightly and holds it against the wind. She is like someone, the young American thinks, whom I have seen, read about, in a story. There is an aureole on her hair, caused by the light reflecting from the brook.

As a child he thought of this brook. It was not where he lived. André stands up suddenly and feels dizzy. Out of his pocket he picks an *image d'épinale.* "Here," he says to the American girl, she was now there, legs of her coming up over the path and the stones, "take this because you're so pretty." "Prends donc cela parce que tu es si belle." Si jolie. For her, this man had an important name: André. André de la Fiscourt. The brook ran past very quickly, and it was not clear to anyone there why it seemed to make them feel so much.

Inside it are a great many small stones. Some of these stay in place for a while and then are moved. Shara picked up a little stone, looking at it. Midwinter, February, and a rather warm day. There was a chill in the air, all the same. There is blood on your face. That's from my razor. He wipes it off. A few miles away Cézanne is painting. The snow melts in the hills and the rain falls down. André gave a purple flower to Dorothy. In the morning, after the storm, there are flowers on the ground. Prends donc cela parce que tu es si belle. The brook runs by. If she were not the American girl he would love her. He loves her because she is. He was terribly excited by her. When the brook is dry, it is the bed of the brook. Ants struggle through it, carrying things which, for their tiny bodies, are enormous. When the paintings are carried into the museum, the brook remains. Sometimes it seems like nothing. I read it and thought about you. The old man's heart is steady. How senseless that André should die. They look at each other.

In the mountains—the hills—the way things happen to the brook are the way things happen in memory. Down here it is something else. André caught his arm with his other hand as he tripped, off balance. Dorothy said Good morning. Tiny particles of liquid constantly evaporate from the stream. This made, sometimes, a haze. The dog ran up to the group. The bird flew away.

The old man didn't see all this. He went away from the brook. He is a living repository of memories. He is Spanish music, never far from the popular echoes of the guitar. He is the novel in which someone is dead. He is another book of poetry.

When she stepped so close to him, his heart fell down. It seemed to. He went looking for it someplace on the ground. She was there, too. He knew what this was about. Music gives a faint reflection, but, unlike the brook, which is content to let everything pass, it uses whatever it has to construct something else. Allons à la maison, let's go to my house. It is right there on top of the hill. It is a very small hill, in fact. And so they go up to it. The brook flows down, in another direction.

3/ The Stone

Sun on the stone. Blond hair beside it. When she gets up, there is sun. He clears the path. The dog runs after the bird. It waits for hours, days, months. Adultery was unheard of at that time. On the path there is a stone. This can be anyone. No harm comes to it. I was lying there, she says, and suddenly I got this idea. Wanted to see you, that's all. The bird flew high, and away. There is a distance of several hundred yards between the terrace with flowers and the stone.

He had some ideas as he took the walk that went past the stone. He is at the telephone. Didn't come to the concert. He is a child compared to the stone. It shows almost no symptoms of change. Some slight flaking, some depetrification is taking place. The old man wept. When the weather changed only slightly, sky grew darker, and bird fell down. It was, near the rock face, moist and humid, but no man or woman was close by. The bird fell into a deserted place. She says I wonder. She had gotten up a long time before.

The stone is a boundary. It may be a headstone when some-one dies. It may be split into various pieces and used in many ways. The girl walked to the desk of the hotel. The stone pointed the way to where the ruins could be seen. It is not itself a ruin in the strictest sense of anything. The plain old stone. His hand on hers was hot. Blood coursing through his veins. I can't go with you, she said. His hand is against the stone. "Why?"

The birds flew over the stone and the clouds flew over the traces of the birds. Above the clouds, at night, there was the silverware of paradise. That is when the stone begins to increase. It has been stable for what seems like eternity. Like everything and everyone else it is the remains of an astonishing original event. The dog is panting—hot. "I—I don't know myself." Later, this changed.

I'm not jealous of anybody, the young man said. That morning the old man woke. He said, Will you see him? I have not seen him for a long time. I am a little jealous. The young woman, the old man, and the young man were all from the same country. The bird flew above it. Shooting white fuzzballs exacerbate the morning summer air. When it is blue tonight—the stone cools. The stone is hot. The young woman brings something small, a package. It is far from the stone. I am not jealous of anybody. There is the stone, the land, and the bird. People made a fuss around it. The girl is wearing white, which goes very well with her blond hair. She holds up one arm in her excitement, in such a way that the wind touches her sleeve and twists it around. Then the chanting begins. A young fly stopped buzzing, long before. To see her tonight. The shadows were tough as though drinking the stone. Stars spit on it.

The stone can easily be imagined to have been there since the beginning, thrown by volcanic force. I hoped you could spend the night. The breath is steady, then flurried and a little sharp. Two hearts pounding. It stays that way for what seems a very long and a very short time. There is fast breathing. She called him gaily over the balustrade. Next month. This year. He walks back and forth. The young woman cries. For some it is a central location.

The dog ran over a path, which was a path of leaves. To one side of the path, about thirty yards from where the dog began, there was a stone. Briefly in the depth images of his eyes, and in the more mysterious images of his olfactory sense, rode the sight and the smell of the stone. And then it was forgotten, completely blank. The old man moves from behind a chaise longue on which the dog has been sitting, chases him off it, and goes out the door. The dog does not follow. He is so restless.

Booming. The construction, still, is over there, unmenacing to the stone. The old man said it was a most unusual Sunday. Usually they were sitting in the restaurant, but today those familiar habits are disturbed.

She takes off her coat and her blouse and her skirt. The weather is warm. The stone sits still. It depends on how old she is. The world revolves. Now it is silent. No one, within human memory, had ever effectively moved it.

4/ The Train

This car cannot be backed up once the others around it start moving. The fir-treed landscape skims away. Books fly this way and that. *The Lace Boxes. A Voyage to the Lands Beyond the Seas. The Indifference of Night and of Sky and of Water.* So it moves, as if destined. Listen, it is half past eleven.

The silver train shines. It descends toward the ocean and runs alongside it. A woman is in a shaded garden, where a white-coated waiter is serving her champagne and she says, "He may have missed the train." She says this to herself. White lace. You see this on her. In the distance, though, you can see the train, its silvery shining.

Jean-Claude walked toward the coast this afternoon with Nina and Henriette and they all three see the train. The train sees nothing, thinks nothing, and does not have to. Fueling, to it, is a necessity. The man enters the compartment—he is twenty-three. Anne is there—a baby.

The phone rang and she went into the house. The room was filled with sunlight. Outside, the house cast a dark, cool shadow. Inside the train there is hurtling and sunlight, shadows and drastic combinations of noises and light. It has been moving for hundreds of miles. The clouds cover the sun but the darkness at this moment might come, also, from the train. Inside there, tables are firmly attached. In the house they move

70

the furniture. The fluffy bird lands. And, at the noise of the train, flies away.

The train wreck causes consternation for miles around. Some people were injured, but not killed. It was not the old man. The sun goes around in the sky. It makes a perfect circle. Not quite. The train goes past.

The woman knew that if she got on the train where she lived, it was capable of taking her elsewhere. The train stayed in the station for a little while. It could be boarded by anyone who had a ticket for it. Once inside it, the places you could go and the directions you could go in were restricted. This was not, though it could seem like, a penalty imposed on you in exchange for the fact that the train was going so rapidly from place to place itself, outside.

When he came to see her, she had written to him. She writes about trains for a school composition. The waiter pours the champagne. The students rush out of their compartments onto the station platform, but he does not appear. Ah, yes, there he is now—Father Desportes! My child! she says, and her little girl runs into the garden. So much human happiness, or the possibility of happiness, in every place to which the train goes.

The little girl isn't on the train. There is another one. She is wearing a white lace dress and is so small she has to be helped up the step that leads to the compartment in which she and her father and her mother are sitting. Or are going to sit. The train moves. It makes a whistling noise. The story of the wheels and the track is writing itself across the country. There is heat between these two, which the tracks lose and the wheels retain. The people inside the train are swallowed by distance. The distance is swallowed by the train. The glasses clink against each other. Is this movement from outside or in? She stands, then sits back down. They were gone, and she was there.

Tremendous pieces of metal soar through the air and then are pounded and soldered together. Almost incredibly, the form of a locomotive appears. She stands up, her face and her

71

white lace dress, too, entirely in shadow. He missed the train. He is there, now, almost at the garden door. After several buckets of champagne, the men smoked long cigars. The train pulled into the station. The train was almost invisible. The train disappeared.

The train went heroically backwards and forwards on its path. Sometimes it hurtled the startled professionals sideways. A baby cried. A mother laughed. A dog barked. The train doesn't last, in its present shape, as long as the stone. It is scrap metal. Some of this is used in new trains, which run along. The train brings the man to the woman. They cry, and hold each other in their arms. A child screams. She laughs. She runs down the hill. At last she does get on it and it goes away.

5/The Book

The book was *The Poems of Guillaume Apollinaire,* translated into English. Then the book was *Alcools.* It has a white paper cover that is slightly smoother and heavier than the pages inside. Each page has a number, and the pages are stuck together. One has to use a knife, or something like it—a sharp postcard will do—to get them apart.

There is a public garden on the postcard, which is lying between two pages of the book *Alcools,* in French, by Apollinaire. When the pages have all been cut, the postcard is put away. The book was sewn and pasted together someplace outside Paris. After it was printed and bound, it was sold. Someone read it who wished to become a saint. Someone read it who said "God damn it!" Someone read it who liked to tear things apart.

The book went everywhere. Though it spoke, it was blind, deaf, mindless, and dumb. It got damp and took a long time to dry off. A baby touches it. Don't! Years later the baby reads the book, but in translation. Then at last the white original is hers. Sitting in the café, smiles. She goes inside.

The city in which she reads the book is the subject of much that is said in the book, but when she raises her eyes she sees the two things, text and city, are very little the same, in fact are totally unlike. An ant walks on the page and is more like the letters on the page. The margin of the page is more like the empty white sky.

The words in the book speak of the city. Her heart beats in her chest. The words do not beat. They are stationary. Apollinaire, sitting in the café on the Place de X, writes the first lines down. Before the book is published these lines may change, or may entirely disappear. He is wearing a white shirt with a loose collar and a blue-gray foulard tied around his neck. He is the writer and she is the woman. Another one is the father, who is also the man. Also, he, the father, writes. Using the back of the book as a table, he writes, "Guillaume Apollinaire." The girl smiles and picks up the unsigned book. The signed book lies on the table. The book is signed. It is unsigned. *Alcools* contains thirty-eight poems. His father had never seen this book, nor his father before him. Nor had the father and grandfather of the woman. Some of these people lived before the poems were written. The book was not published.

Apollinaire was not born. Now he is in existence. The girl picks up the book and opens it at random. "Annie," "Cortège," "La Chanson du mal aimé." The words lie flat on the page. Not quite completely flat but almost. It reappears, in fresh white new stiff clothes, new covers and paper. When it is worn, they decide whether or not to replace it. The book falls on a step and is immediately picked up.

André gives the book to Dorothy. She is unable to read it. The young woman sits in the café. The weather is gray, and even at a short distance things become dim. The old man smiles at her. The rain is falling. She stands up. She wipes some water off the book. He is now a rather young man. May I help you into the taxi. Thank you. Their housemaids clean away the plates and the glasses. A horn sounds. Smoke comes out of the chimney. Apollinaire is born. The mother is nervous. Have you read this book?

The book is printed by a large firm. The roof of the building does not slant. Inside there is the noise of printing presses. *Alcools* emerges from these machines. This book lies on a table. This book is in a young girl's hand. Another book is by Éluard, another by Max Jacob.

The man and the young woman embrace. She says "I can't" and then "I can." The book doesn't move. In the café the book is with someone else. It is autumn. He goes past. Apollinaire writes "Cortège." Children run out of a graveyard and dance. Colors are spread out across windows. A garden filled with roses and a villa which is like a rose. All this is in the book. In the restaurant. The smoke and the service and the smiles and the clutching of hands. Nothing can separate us now. He loved her, but she was unable to love him back. "I don't know why."

From the book ideas fall like snowflakes over foreheads at the cafés bent over the problems of creating a modern classic. The classic forms instantly. Like a newspaper. Coffee is steaming in the cups. He pays for the book and leaves the store.

Where are you going. The book flies into her bag. I am late. Smell of cinammon. When will you call me. It is held together by tightly sewn threads, and it lies on the table. Apollinaire's experience is inside the book, in a strange form: printed letters —capital and small ones—commas, periods, dashes, spaces. On top of each poem are letters slightly larger than those inside it. Tomorrow, the young woman laughed—and she tossed back her hair. Later he picks it up and begins to read.

6/ The Music

When the woman heard the music, it was not for the first time. Nor was this the first woman, nor was it the first woman who ever heard the music. The letter arrives with the tickets. We must get dressed up! The white gloves, the shoes, and the sidewalks will carry us. There were five men, or four men and one woman. White neckties hit white shirts, while to either side a neat curving line of black velvet descends. The violin starts, and then there is the sound of a piano. One man and one woman went into the hotel. Today we have a special performance—of Mozart's Quartet for Strings and Piano, Köchel listing 493.

This is the day that Dorothy goes to the concert. André goes. The musicians perform. They do not wear white gloves. Their music is on the page. It is by them picked or strung or brushed or blown into their instruments, and it leaps out, at each second, totally changed.

From far away there is nothing. When you are close to the building, some faint sounds are hearable from inside. Insects are singing. The concert has been planned for months, was organized last year. The music is by Mozart.

She invited them to go with her to the concert. The old bent woman in black clothing walked past the concert. The concert was at nine o'clock. Another is at three. Music was played in the hall. The old man at the concert did not know the old woman who was walking by. She was a new character in the story, and she lived in the mountains. The music slipped out of the instruments and glided away. The men who play the instruments went after it, with their fingers and their mouths, and brought it back. At the hotel, across the street, it is very quiet, and the man and woman look at each other. The music was by Mozart, his Quartet for Strings and Piano, Köchel 493.

An old woman in a lace dress leans forward to tap on the wood of the piano with her fan. November, seventeen sixty-two. Mozart is very young. He wears white knickers with a gold-colored belt. His wrists touched by sleeves, his head tossed back, he sits at the piano.

Two hundred concertgoers are in this auditorium. One of them is a man who was once attacked by a bear in a city zoo. His shoulder still shows scars where the animal's claws dug into him. He was forced to stay in the hospital for a long time. An undertaker is also at the concert. And Shara is there. And one hundred and ninety-seven others. Many "society" ladies are among them. Some of them love music. For others the concert hall is a fashionable place to go. Their dogs are at home, rambling through the furniture. The maid chases one of them off a settee. No, Boxer, you mustn't! The sea decorates its eyelids with piers and stars as the fantastic night in Istanbul breaks through the historical webbing, as a story is broken through by its writing, and as the music is broken through by the fact that it is a concert at which there are two hundred people and the sound of the instruments is of fibre and wood. Something takes the shape of an animal, is about to attack him, draws a valentine in the little girl's mind. How does she happen to be at the concert? Her father is there. Some woman is introducing herself as her mother. What did you say they were going to play? I don't know. The music cannot get through to the Turkish Ambassador. The girl has to relax very hard to make the Mozart decorate the valentine in the way she thinks she wants it to. Some things are too sweet to be named. The future seems there in her consciousness. When she lives, it is the present all the time. He was sitting in a middle row and she near the front. At first they don't see each other. Later they do.

When you were going to the concert, you got all dressed up. White satin blouse, black silk skirt, alligator handbag, and off you go. She powders her nose. The music begins. The violins go very far, then the viola comes, the bass, and then the piano. It is like a brook, rippling. It moves around. The woman is at home. He is at the concert. The bird does not see him. The apricot tree is in blossom. Her cheekbone appears. The man lies down next to his dog. Waking up, the woman was surprised by the music. The young man felt overwhelmed by it.

Dorothy loved music. She loved it more than anything else except André. There are several white limed statues on the hill. The old man did not come to this concert. Shara did, however. She had never gone back to India, as it was originally planned that she would. Nor did the American boy marry her. The concert was scheduled to begin at two o'clock. There were many people who were unable to attend.

The mother sings to the baby. Her song has one quality of the music. She doesn't believe it is exactly that which she wants. There is a definite pleasure in this, but in the Mozart there is more. She has to find someone to stay with the children. Her mother comes in. She had loved the old man as much as life, as breath. The music begins. The music begins again. At each moment she was able again to listen the music was beginning. She would have to learn to listen to music better. He would have to learn to live without her. He would have to learn to live with her. The composer has his work. The people are scattered about. They were both smiling, too. The incredibly sweet sounds of the violins stopped. The little girl —where is her valentine? Perhaps, her mother says, you left it on the train. The old woman wasn't looking—she walked right into the path of a car. Father Desportes ran over to the garden where the citizens were waiting for the mayor to speak. Come quickly! he cried. The concert is going to begin. Ideally, the music would have shown all these people how to live, taught them a harmony they could master in their own lives. Its elements, however, were so different from the elements of their lives—even its terms—*andante, stretto, largo,* and the rest— that it was impossible for it to do that. It seemed to some to suggest a paradise they couldn't have. This was only, of course, if it was viewed as leading to something other than itself.

7/ The Woman and the Man

In the room there is a chair, a mirror, a window, and a bed. The woman takes off her blouse and the man approaches her. Many years before, the sun shone through the trees and the brook ran across the pasture. The woman is someone he has never seen.

When they placed their hands on each other's bodies, it seemed strange to think of anything else. They were not always doing that. Since, however, it gave more pleasure than any-thing else they did, they never could decide how often to do it, when to do it and when not.

The man was the conductor of the orchestra at a concert and the man who killed the bird. The woman was the young woman who had loved the old man. The statue of Diana was the model of the form of the woman, and the statue of Apollo the model of the form of the man. When the old man saw these statues, he cried. He had never learned how to accept such a thing. The old man is the man and the young woman is the woman. The Mayan woman is the woman. The Mayan man is the man. The sun shines on the dead shoulder of the man. The shoulder regains life and it moves. The wall is neither the woman nor the man, but with grass and with insects, and the wind in it, it is alive. The life in the wall dies down and the weather turns cold. The woman screams. The man shouts, and the boat comes in toward the dock.

The man places his hand on the woman's shoulder. The street runs backward from where you are. Eventually you do not care what anyone thinks. If it is a street, it is there for you to walk on. The woman takes the man's arm and they go away.

The man wakes up first. The woman saw the bird. When she went back to sleep, the man was gone. The man was Apollo. The woman was made of stone. Apollo said, "If you are stone, then stone shall be my stair." He placed his arms around the woman. The stone became a step. The woman places her hand on the man's shoulder. He too is made of stone.

They are flesh and blood, warm-hearted and humorous. They laugh. The man takes the woman's hand. He takes her hand and they go walking. They walk a very long way. They walk past the place where the piano was. They walk past the stone. The dog saw the man before the bird did who flew away. Apollo took out his gun and aimed it at the sky.

The stone that went into making the statues for a long time resisted the hands of the sculptor. But she does not resist him, nor he her. They, however, make nothing of each other. It is as individuals that they exist, for anyone else. Whatever André said to Dorothy (he could not remember it now) it was certainly about their being the woman and the man. It was not about their being the statues. The old man writes in a journal. The sun streaked yellow over the hills, and the window of the car was open through which she poked her head. Listen, do you want to come to the concert. André looked at the brook. The child who had played with the stone will never see him again. When he came home she had changed into a yellow dress and shoes. He was a statue and she leaned against him. When the woman and the man came out, there was a baby, who didn't know what to do. Later on, they thought, although they said nothing, that the baby would know, just as they did now. The baby would know how to be big and not to be a statue.

André is the man and Hélène is the woman. It is Dorothy. Hello. She leans against him. She is made of velvet. He is a greeting card, white and red and gold. There is a gilded glimmering all about them. On the other side of the card are some words. "Congratulations on Your Marriage." In the comic strip the man looks a long way away and in the next square you see the woman is coming. In the film the woman and the man embrace. Embarrassed, he turned away. She raises the window, and there are words: "Bonne fête."

Together, they like to speak. "You make me very happy." "What did I ever do when I was alone?" "Who are you, really?" "What did life mean without you?" "What time are you coming?" "How would you like my hair?" "My sleeves?" "My boots?" "Give me a little time." "All right, I'm ready." "So it's really you!" The old man saw the statues and cried.

She carries a shopping bag, he a parcel. Inside the parcel is something that can be cut into ribbons. Inside her shopping bag is the marble head of a Cupid. This bag is too heavy. The music plays, and she puts it down. He picks it up. She is gone. The parcel is blue, green, and white ribbons. The shopping bag rustles. The head of Cupid flies out. But it is not that. It is the bird. So it seems. Apollo fires the gun and the man falls. When he gets up again, with sunlight shining in his eyes, the woman is gone. Instead of the man there is the woman. Instead of the bird there is stone.

You must come to the concert. Oh, I will. The statues of Diana and Apollo stand in the field. This is a park. Before it is a park, it is nothing, wild nature. Before that, it is molten lava and gas.

Dawn finds the woman and the man together and wrings her hands. Too late! Lascivious behavior! You should be up! The man gets up. The woman gets up. Together they go back to bed. The slate roof of a low building edges out over the poured concrete of the sidewalk in a recently rebuilt part of the city. They pay tribute to each other with a cup of coffee. The woman dresses. The man dresses the woman. She undresses the man, finding that he is Apollo. He is made of water, air, and stone. She is made, seemingly, of lilacs, anise, and sea foam. The man is not Aphrodite, the man is Zeus. The woman is Aphrodite. The bedroom is the ocean. The window is Botticelli.

The man is Apollo. At the sound of the music they become more themselves. The old man signals to the dog that it is time to run out. Let me show you this book. Too sweet to be named. The city seems "lazy." The country stretches out. They are gods. Out of what is simple something complex has been made. When they touch each other, they are unconscious of where they are. He is the man and she is the woman. He is the young Frenchman and she is the American girl. This takes place in the city. When she touches him, she finds he is made of stone. No god fired the rifle. She takes his arm.

8/ This Story

The characters are the old man, who is in fact two or three different persons, and the young man, who the old man once was, and another young man, and a few others, such as André, and the young man who is the son of the family in the house with the step and who may be the one who killed the bird. There is the father, the man who loved the woman with the piano, and there is the man on the train, who loved the woman in white lace. The women are Shara, Dorothy, and Hélène, the woman in white lace, and the young woman who read the book, and the woman in The Woman and the Man. Among the other actors are Diana, Apollo, the dog, the bird, Guillaume Apollinaire, and Paul Cézanne. A girl is hanging up the laundry. I am writing. It is a year, nineteen seventy-eight. A month, March. A time of day, afternoon, or it is the late part of morning. It is a light, dark. Or rather dark white light. The old man yawns, and the young woman puts on a dress that is very clean, just washed and ironed an instant ago, and in that same instant it didn't quite yet exist. Now it does and may always exist. This is like the music of Mozart, like the effect it has. The girl runs out of the house. Now the old man feels dead.

He revives at the concert, though, the very next day. It is five o'clock in the afternoon. When the old man meets her at the train she is carrying a light yellow umbrella. These are very strong feelings. Still, as in the Mozart, they are together.

There is the story of how the story was written. It was inspired by a concert of music by Mozart, specifically by his Quartet for Strings and Piano, Köchel 493. The concert hall was in Rome. In the hall, leading up to the place where the orchestra sat and played, was a green step. He had never seen this before. The music created something else in him, in his imagination. The rest of life was not blocked out, but the music made him see and feel green fields and the freshness of everything, people and stones. By repetition, by melody, by recurring sounds which in a way made no point outside themselves, he came, almost instantly, to a vision of nature, a vision of life as being enough in itself, fresh, exacting, firm as a stone, unambiguous, unexaggerated, recurring, and free. It is a version perhaps, the simplest he had ever seen, of paradise.

Sitting at the typewriter, light coming in windows, blood

going through the arteries and the veins—the past delighting in itself was far in the distance—melodies become opaque— a man, seemingly a waiter, in a slightly soiled white suit, approaches him with a tray. Signore, would you like your tray? The old man dies. He is born again, in a fortnight. The light changes. The weather changes. The dog's fur changes, but later in the cycle of warm and cold. This palace dates from the sixteenth century. It was constructed then. The tin can outside the window, the cloth-bound books inside.

Inside him Provence is illuminated, and the Boulevard Raspail, what is the name of that huge hotel? And the rue du Cherche-Midi. However—he shuts down the typewriter with a bang. Where is my dinner? Where, for God's sake, is my lunch? Who really owns the Vatican? What is going on outside?

In the Mozart concert the notes went high above the green step, circled, and came down. They gave an impression of continuing and of being connected not only to one another but also to everything else. Will there ever be enough time? Time to do all that is suggested? In ordinary life, no. And to make it into something else is to go beyond.

The story is written and is rewritten and it blows about. It furnishes an apartment. Its oddness is apparent. There is a part about a house in the country, near Aix, with a lawn sloping, and a driveway, a stairway, and a garden. The cork was in a bottle of white wine in a restaurant, on a hill, with terraces, and there the woman in white lace was sitting and waiting for a man. One table was in Paris in a café, almost identical with the table on which the young woman puts down the book, and the table to which the waiter walked, and the other was a table on a hillside near Aix-en-Provence where someone is selling (was selling) little things to eat. "The Pain" became "The Pleasure and the Pain." Its quality changes, and finally it sleeps. The author is the old man, the young man, the young woman, Shara, the green step, the ocean, the city, and the girl. He is all the women. He is the men. He is the statues eternally in union as in disunion. He is the sheets of paper floating above the room. I sit down to write. The woman reads the story. She knows that the author is the old man when he was somewhat younger. He, too, is unable to finish anything. Instead he begins to write about what he has already written. He hears the Mozart. These are very strong feelings to have been suggested by a green step, by a concert, by anything. The laundress hangs things up to dry. Whatever this cost, it is worth it. After a while, of course, it ends up only as part of a book.

The story takes place in Aix-en-Provence, a large part of it. The other largest part takes place in Paris. A small part, the larger part of this last part, takes place in Rome. The reality of objects and sensations in one place combines with psychological availability in another. Recent happiness and present unhappiness mix and unmix and mix. Traffic. Women are a great part for the old man but not everything. If only he had read more books. The young woman hands him the book by Guillaume Apollinaire. "You will learn nothing from this one but about some feelings in your life. It's a reflection of, more than part of, the substance of human wisdom." When the bird was shot, the young woman's piano struck a chord and the shining train went past. The stone remained where it was and is, it could hardly have imagined what was thought and written. The brook darted onwards, and André smiled. Already it was a slightly chilly day. The green step was free of encumbrances. Now there is a shoe's bottom on it and now not, as the concert group begins to play. Is everything included? Shall I take you as far as the bus? The man and the woman are saying good-bye. They have the characteristic of movement, which is the supreme utilization of time.

About the Author

KENNETH KOCH's other books of poetry include *The Burning Mystery of Anna in 1951*, *The Duplications*, *The Art of Love*, *The Pleasures of Peace*, *Thank You and Other Poems* and *Ko, or A Season on Earth*. He is also the author of a book of plays, *A Change of Hearts;* a novel, *The Red Robins;* and four books on education—*Wishes, Lies, and Dreams; Rose, Where Did You Get That Red?; I Never Told Anybody;* and *Sleeping on the Wing* (with Kate Farrell). He lives in New York City and is Professor of English at Columbia University.